POEMS
OF
RESISTANCE

**Marc
Thomas**

ISBN: 979-8-9925811-3-3

Human Authored™, Reg #: 5193396,
https://authorsguild.org/human

SAVANNAH, GA

2025

POEMS
OF
RESISTANCE

DEDICATION

to the victims of injustice
and the workers for justice
anytime
anywhere
but especially
here and now

TABLE OF CONTENTS

POEMS OF RESISTANCE

i am not brave, or strong
but i am
concerned
afraid
dismayed
angry
and i cannot be quiet

WHAT IS TO BE DONE?

in troubled times
this question
has been asked, and asked again,
and it must now be asked again
today i wondered
what is poetry for?
or rather,
what is my poetry for?
and
what is to be done?
day to day
in all the little details of my life?
and i think back
and realize
that i was first radicalized
by books -
by poems and novels
often old ones
but with messages still new
with examples still strong
which is why they burn books
why even the books
in the imaginary canon
are often at risk
and i think back

and browse my shelves
and realize that the answer
to the question
What Is To Be Done?
is the same as always
do not comply
do not give them power
do not be afraid
for they fear nothing more
than the unafraid
and words have power, so
love the world
notice the beauty, the good, the kind
and speak out joyfully
about the need to be free
think freely
read freely
speak freely
write freely
and be unafraid

WAR OF WORDS

it is a war for language
for free speech
and for clear meanings

for poets
the right words
the best words
are breath and life

and we know
we work every day
with their depth and breadth
their resonances
their baggage
their deep anchors
in memories
and cultures

and so we must resist
when speech is sanitized
stripped down
pushed up against the wall
and told to behave
or be jailed

of course
we all know
that speech, and poems,
can be weaponized

after all,
we too fight
with and for our words -
so we must not degrade them

do not return hate with hate
do not answer lies with lies
strike for the weak points
call bullshit

but do not exaggerate
this war
will be for the long run
and must be won
by clarity
and depth
not a wallow in mud

PURGING TRUTHS

my internet is ill
my computer fails me
my search engines are ailing
they have lost their strength
they cannot find what they used to find
and serve me up pretensions -
substitutes for truths

they have purged
their diversity
the algorithms
are not more intelligent
but more artificial
pushing all responses
into desired conformity

they are purging equity
the fight for fairness
for equal rights
is being taken out and beaten in the alley
the museums and libraries
are being forced
into a perverse mythology

they are avoiding inclusiveness
deviation is criminalized
oddities are expunged

the joy of variety
of challenging innovation
of celebratory absurdity
of the invention of new ways
to be your new self
are being locked in the closets

they are complying in advance
and denying the truth
they will fail

always, and forever,
we must change to live -
all new "endless forms most beautiful"
are branched off
by original variations

grow
change
blossom
by a new truth
spread your words

ANTICIPATORY COMPLIANCE

i learned a new phrase this week
"anticipatory compliance"
it comes from business,
especially those businesses
who practice careful risk management
who want to avoid
losses
lawsuits
regulators
public shame
or any public trouble at all
and it should mean
know the rules
and follow them
do what you are supposed to do
keep good records
be trustworthy
and above all,
be honest
but,
and this is a big but,
it has come to mean
court the inspectors
be careful what you write down
look out for the camera
destroy the evidence
hire good lawyers

don't get caught
but if you do
deny, lie, deny
or
for the public
which is relatively powerless
it means
keep your head down
stay out of trouble
and above all,
be afraid,
be very afraid,
don't rock the boat,
and don't put your head up and look around

to which,
i call bullshit -
do not comply

SPEAK FREELY

to be free
you must act free
you must not be afraid to speak

yes
words are powerful
and they can do great damage
and words
in certain circumstances
can be crimes

so
you must speak carefully
with regard to risk and consequences
but
do not be silent out of fear
speak fairly
and speak out

if you see abuse
name it
if you see crime
call it out
if you hear lies
rebut them

and
if you are told you are wrong
listen
for the demand for freedom
creates the responsibility for tolerance
and for listening
because
unfortunately
we cannot be right
all the time

and your listening creates
a complementary demand
to be listened to
so use it
to speak
often, clearly, fearlessly
and be heard

TROUBLE

you think you know trouble?

let me tell you about trouble -
trouble is not
feeling miserable
lonely or bored
stifled at a job

bad trouble is when
the grand jury throws your ass in jail
for refusing to rat out
your neighbor or your friend

bad trouble is losing
your job
your dog
your apartment
all your possessions
your friend

trouble follows you
trouble is a constant
there is no
smooth and blessed life
no isle of happiness

but trouble is not
your self-respect
your knowing right from wrong
your willingness to fight

yes,
trouble is a constant

but there is good trouble
and the fight for justice
is a struggle eternal
and
this battle has just begun

NAZI

how do you hear this?
what does it mean?
how does it make you feel?
what do you see?

this word weapon
illuminates little
obscures much
is often misused
but sometimes
in hard times
in desperate times
it is the only right word

do not confuse it
with the newsreel images
of symbols that may or may not be
meaningful
it does not mean
jackboots and soldiers
it does not mean
stiff armed salutes
it does not mean
rants and ravings
to worshiping crowds

it does not always mean
and certainly does not only mean
hatred of Jews
the elevation of the ignorant

it does mean
contempt for the many
the love of power
simply for power's sake
the authority of few
the hate of some others
libeled and stigmatized others
the manipulation of fears
the demonization of opponents
and
denial of inconvenient facts

it comes in disguise
wearing suits
with eloquent speech
good educations
careful legal arguments
suppression of critics
disregard for law
resistance to openness
and
contempt for those

whom they consider
weak, undesirable,
or simply other

above all,
it elevates the few
and allows no value
for the poor,
the ill, the unlucky,
the old,
or,
worst of all,
the unusual

so learn this word
keep it available
but do not misuse it
do not abuse it -
for when it is used
too early, too often
it loses its sting
but save it
keep it ready
a word weapon
for when it is needed -

for times like these

NEVER UNDERESTIMATE THEM

when i wake up in the morning
i give in to temptation
and let the mockery on social media
arouse me and raise me up

but then i remember -
never underestimate your enemy
it is too easy to distract ourselves
by making jokes

when you vilify
when you mock as fools and clowns
when you disparage
the intelligence and judgment
of those whom you should fear
you open yourself to error

you may relieve yourself, reduce your fears,
release anxiety in laughter
but beware

remember
you cannot fight lies with lies
the best defense against half truths
is not mockery
but the whole truth

mock the leaders to weaken them
but mock them best in their own words
attack their contradictions
find their hypocrisies
reveal their self interests

don't mock their followers just for following
do not assume they are stupid
just because you think they are mistaken
they know where the library is
most of them read as much as you do
(but not the same things)

be particular
don't make assumptions
do not answer rudeness with rudeness
but call out the rude
film the violent
document the hypocrites
greet hatefulness
with openness

fight their leaders
but, when you can,
be merciful to their followers

hear them
listen
listen for the fear

respect their losses
even the imagined ones
and
ask them why
they disrespect you

it is hard
to be patient
so
think of it as
stubbornness
not politeness
persistence
not mercy
resistance
not concurrence

resistance
is not always
a lightning bolt
or a flood -
sometimes
it must be glacial

so
mock and laugh
to get up in the morning
to weaken the vain and the mighty
to find relief

to share solidarity -
but
never, never
think it is enough

mockery may weaken
but it does not defeat
do not indulge in contempt
for that risks underestimation
and that serves the enemy

resist
speak freely
write freely

support,
above all,
the resistance
of the bravest among us
and help them
speak, write, and act
freely

there is a cancer in our country
and it is at the top
in the worship of wealth
the glorification of the few
the theft of power
by a minority

and it must be removed

so,
when they come to you
asking
suggesting
requiring
ordering
you
to do what you know is wrong
do not comply

but never underestimate them

A GIFT FOR YOU

do you really need things?
the catalogs have little
that would truly
offer you a blessing,
nothing holy,
little good,
though much that plays at piety or virtue

instead of things,
the best i can offer you
is your freedom
to be good
and act well in the world

first,
we must cast aside
The Ten Commandments:
five statements about power,
plus five prohibitions -

neither prayers nor ideologies
neither right opinion
nor ritual purity
truly do good,
or change the world,
but actions do

second,
practice
the necessary and sacred
acts of compassion,
the only gifts worth giving,
helping others,
to being willing to give

practice these:
feed the hungry,
give drink to the thirsty,
clothe the naked,
shelter the homeless,
care for the sick,
aid the imprisoned,
bury the dead,
teach the ignorant,
give books to the curious,
speak freely,
challenge the certain

these are sufficient.
the Kingdom of Heaven
is within you

STRATEGY AND TACTICS

if
you are going to resist

you need a plan

and, to make a plan,
you need to
set objectives
commit resources
assess risks
establish your loss tolerance
form a strategy
and choose your tactics

and that's where thought
and wishful thinking
and your outrage
get turned into action -
or not

the good thing is
it's clear right now
that there are no monolithic powers
just wannabes

the bad thing is
it's clear right now
that all bases of resistance
are divided
because there is no overall vision or plan

this is where
you focus your objectives -
fight the great powers?
(confused, inept, and contradictory though
they be)
or
fight for the purity of your vision?
or
fight the divisions of the resistance?

you may have more than one objective
but ONE must dominate

and you must choose your role -
are you joining a resistance?
or leading one,
if only locally.

most of us will join one,
and rightly so
for the fire and vision of leadership
are hard to bear
and rarely satisfied

so, collect intelligence -
who is doing what,
and
are they
visionary purists
angry citizens
driven by oppressed identity
and who do you like?
who can you work with?

for you are a resource
and it is okay for your plan
to be to join an other's plan

then assess
what are you willing to pay?

your time?
your words?
your face and voice?
are you willing to argue with
and listen to
the supporters of the opposition?
give money?
stand on the front line?
accept tear gas or a battering?
arrest and detention?
the costs of lawyers?

your life?
someone else's life?

there is no one right answer
for you
except the one you make
and follow through

HOW DO YOU STAND?

it is hard
to act
to speak
not to act
to stay silent

so much evil
is done so far away
to people we don't know

it is so easy
to turn back to our lives
comfortable, here and now

when hungry children
are shot for being hungry
and in the wrong place and time
and born to the wrong parents

when people die or starve
because people in Washington
have stopped the flow of money
that had been a source of life

when our government takes sides
in a conflict far away
that is timeless and endless

and shows no hope of conclusion
and no chance of diplomacy

when the leaders of nations
wring their hands, have conferences,
and write condemning memos
yet stop short
of turning their words into actions

are we guilty
if we take no action
and do not speak?

do we lack compassion
if we stand quietly
helpless and hopeless?

answer for yourself

THE QUESTION OF VIOLENCE

i do not propose violence
i do not support violence
here and now
but
the question is there

when commitment is passionate
when resistance is crushed
when power is based
on policies of death

is violence justified?

face it -
right or left,
anarchist or fascist,
god-drunk or god-hater
patriot or revolutionary,
violence
has often been seized
as the final
the necessary
the honorable
even the holy
choice

and i cannot say

it has always been wrong
that all of the violent were evil
that none of the violent were heroes

right now
some places in this world
there are heroes
violent and willing to die
to save others
to save the future
to save their people
and their children

i salute them
i support them

but
for me
here and now
it is not the time
not yet

but sometimes my clock is wrong

AT LEAST

agreed

as individuals
we are weak
divided
have other obligations
are
conflicted
compromised

but

at least,
if you have any compassion
speak
and speak to the point

if you cannot comfort the afflicted
because
they are too many
or too far away
at least,
afflict the comfortable

afflict
those around you
those who represent you

those who claim to speak for you
and serve your interests
and make sure
that they bear their share of shame

as for us,
here, in our homes and times,
we may be distressed
we may be angry

but do not delude yourself
at least
admit it
we are not innocent

BUT WHAT CAN I DO?

you and i are not heroes
or charismatic leaders

but there are many of us
and many of us
are working for good

just get out there
and look for people
you can work with

join in
numbers count -
just ask the ants

show up
write emails
go to meetings
go to rallies
answer phones
make phone calls
write poems
talk to your friends
listen to your neighbors
and then
talk to them

above all
aid the victims
raise up
those being
ground down
pushed out
in these troubled times

just remember
you need to keep your balance
between
the wisdom of groups
and the madness of crowds

KNOW YOUR RIGHTS

[From the American Civil Liberties Union Website: https://www.aclu.org/know-your-rights]

If Police Stop You in Public

Your rights

- You have the right to remain silent. For example, you do not have to answer any questions about where you are going, where you are traveling from, what you are doing, or where you live. If you wish to exercise your right to remain silent, say so out loud. (In some states, you may be required to provide your name if asked to identify yourself, and an officer may arrest you for refusing to do so.)
- You do not have to consent to a search of yourself or your belongings, but police may pat down your clothing if they suspect a weapon. Note that refusing consent may not stop the officer from carrying out the search against your will, but making a timely

objection before or during the search
can help preserve your rights in any
later legal proceeding.
- If you are arrested by police, you have
the right to a government-appointed
lawyer if you cannot afford one.
- You do not have to answer questions
about where you were born, whether
you are a U.S. citizen, or how you
entered the country. (Separate rules
apply at international borders and
airports as well as for individuals on
certain nonimmigrant visas, including
tourists and business travelers. For
more specific guidance about how to
deal with immigration-related
questions, see the section on immigrant
rights below.)

How to reduce risk to yourself

- Stay calm. Don't run, resist, or obstruct
the officers. Do not lie or give false
documents. Keep your hands where the
police can see them.

What to do if you are arrested or detained

- Say you wish to remain silent and ask for a lawyer immediately. Don't give any explanations or excuses. Don't say anything, sign anything, or make any decisions without a lawyer.
- If you have been arrested by police, you have the right to make a local phone call. The police cannot listen if you call a lawyer. They can and often do listen if you call anyone else.

If you believe your rights were violated

- Write down everything you remember, including officers' badges and patrol car numbers, which agency the officers were from, and any other details. Get contact information for witnesses.
- If you're injured, seek medical attention immediately and take photographs of your injuries.
- File a written complaint with the agency's internal affairs division or civilian complaint board. In most cases,

you can file a complaint anonymously if you wish.

What you can do if you think you're witnessing police abuse or brutality

- Stand at a safe distance and, if possible, use your phone to record video of what is happening. As long as you do not interfere with what the officers are doing and do not stand close enough to obstruct their movements, you have the right to observe and record events that are plainly visible in public spaces.
- Do not try to hide the fact that you are recording. Police officers do not have a reasonable expectation of privacy when performing their jobs, but the people they are interacting with may have privacy rights that would require you to notify them of the recording. In many states (see here) you must affirmatively make people aware that you are recording them.
- Police officers may not confiscate or demand to view your photographs or

video without a warrant, and they may not delete your photographs or video under any circumstances. If an officer orders you to stop recording or orders you to hand over your phone, you should politely but firmly tell the officer that you do not consent to doing so, and remind the officer that taking photographs or video is your right under the First Amendment. Be aware that some officers may arrest you for refusing to comply even though their orders are illegal. The arrest would be unlawful, but you will need to weigh the personal risks of arrest (including the risk that officer may search you upon arrest) against the value of continuing to record.

- Whether or not you are able to record everything, make sure to write down everything you remember, including officers' badge and patrol car numbers, which agency the officers were from, how many officers were present and what their names were, any use of weapons (including less-lethal weapons such as Tasers or batons), and any injuries suffered by the person stopped. If you are able to speak to the person stopped by police after the police leave, they may find your contact information helpful in case they decide to file a complaint or pursue a lawsuit against the officers.

If You Are an Immigrant and Police Stop You

How to reduce risk to yourself

- Stay calm. Don't run, argue, resist, or obstruct the officer, even if you believe your rights are being violated. Keep your hands where police can see them.
- Don't lie about your status or provide false documents.

Your rights

- You have the right to remain silent and do not have to discuss your immigration or citizenship status with police, immigration agents, or other officials. Anything you tell an officer can later be used against you in immigration court.

- If you are not a U.S. citizen and an immigration agent requests your immigration papers, you must show them if you have them with you.
- If an immigration agent asks if they can search you, you have the right to say no. Agents do not have the right to search you or your belongings without your consent or probable cause.
- If you're over 18, carry your papers with you at all times. If you don't have them, tell the officer that you want to remain silent, or that you want to consult a lawyer before answering any questions.

What to do in such an encounter

- In some states, you must provide your name to law enforcement if you are stopped and told to identify yourself. But even if you give your name, you don't have to answer other questions.
- If you are driving and are pulled over, the officer can require you to show your

license, vehicle registration and proof of
insurance, but you don't have to answer
questions about your immigration
status.

- Customs officers can ask about your
immigration status when entering or
leaving the country. If you are a lawful
permanent resident (LPR) who has
maintained your status, you only have
to answer questions establishing your
identity and permanent residency.
Refusal to answer other questions will
likely cause delay, but officials may not
deny you entry into the United States
for failure to answer other questions. If
you are a non-citizen visa holder, you
may be denied entry into the U.S. if you
refuse to answer officers' questions.

The website of the American Civil Liberties
Union also has useful information about
talking to people about their rights, and the
rights of:

Abortion supporters and providers
Digital rights
Dreamers

LGBTQ+ rights
Prisoner rights
Religious freedom
Student rights
Voting rights

BIBLIOGRAPHY

Civil Disobedience by Henry David Thoreau

The Rights of Man by Thomas Paine

The Origins of Totalitarianism by Hannah Arendt

On Tyranny: Twenty Lessons from the Twentieth Century by Timothy Snyder

On Freedom by Timothy Snyder

The Anatomy of Fascism by Robert O. Paxton

On Lying and Politics by Hannah Arendt

Rules for Radicals by Saul Alinsky

March by John Lewis

A Testament of Hope: the Essential Writings and Speeches by Martin Luther King, Jr.

Why Civil Resistance Works: The Strategic Logic of Nonviolent Conflict by Erica Chenoweth and Maria Stephan

and many, many more